**Susanne Tayfoor**

 W9-BGI-432

Common mistakes at

First Certificate

... and how to avoid them

CAMBRIDGE UNIVERSITY PRESS
Cambridge, New York, Melbourne, Madrid, Cape Town, Singapore, São Paulo

Cambridge University Press
The Edinburgh Building, Cambridge CB2 2RU, UK

www.cambridge.org
Information on this title: www.cambridge.org/9780521520621

© Cambridge University Press 2004

This publication is in copyright. Subject to statutory exception
and to the provisions of relevant collective licensing agreements,
no reproduction of any part may take place without the written
permission of Cambridge University Press.

First published 2004
4th printing 2005

Printed in Italy by Legoprint S.p.A.

A catalogue record for this publication is available from the British Library

ISBN-13 978-0-521-52062-1 paperback
ISBN-10 0-521-52062-2 paperback

Contents

Can I use the future after *when* or *if*? *No ?*

1 Tick the correct sentence in each pair.

1 ✓a When she starts her new job she'll get a company car.
  b When she'll start her new job she'll get a company car.
2 ✓a If you miss the train you'll have to take a taxi.
  b If you will miss the train you'll have to take a taxi.

If and *when* can link two parts of a sentence.
We often use the present simple directly after these
words, even though we are talking about the future:
When I retire, *I'll travel round the world.*

The same thing happens when we use *before, after,
until, by the time* and *as soon as*:
*I'll phone you **as soon as I arrive**.*
By the time we get *home, it will be dark.*
We can use *will* after *when* if we use *when* as a
question word:
When will *I see you again?*

2 Correct the mistake below.

I'll be surprised if she will pass her exams!

I .__ll..be...... surprised ..if....she.......passes... her exams!

3 Complete the sentences below using the correct form of the verbs.

1 If you ......treat...... *(treat)* her so unfairly she'll walk out of the job.
2 Could you phone me when .you..have. *(you / have)* the results of the test?
3 By the time they ...arrive..... *(arrive)* the match will be over.
4 If Kathy ......gets...... *(get)* in touch next week, I'll let you know.
5 Let's go out for a drink after we ...finish..... *(finish)* these accounts.
6 I don't like unexpected visitors, so I hope she rings before she ...arrives... *(arrive)*!
7 You can't drive a car in England until you ...are......... *(be)* seventeen.
8 You .... *(have to / retake)* the exam if you ....fail...... *(fail)* it.
       will have to retake

5

How do I use present tenses to talk about the future?

1 Tick the correct sentence in each pair.

1 (a) Sara won't be able to come; she's going skiing next weekend.
  ✗ b Sara won't be able to come; she'll go skiing next weekend.
2 ✓(a) Can you tell me what time the next train leaves?
  b Can you tell me what time the next train will leave?

Several different future forms are possible, but in general we most commonly use the present continuous to talk about an arrangement:
I'm taking my exam tomorrow!

We use *will* for instant reactions, predictions and promises:
That's the doorbell! I'll get it!

Compare:
- *I'll probably stay in tomorrow night.* (I've got no arranged plans)
- *I'm playing squash tomorrow night.* (I've already arranged it)

We use the present simple for future timetabled events.
Compare:
- *The plane leaves at 8 am.* (timetabled event)
- *I'm leaving the house at 5.30 am.* (personal arrangement)

2 Correct the mistake below.

Tonight we'll have a surprise party for Gemma's birthday!

Tonight ...*we are having a surprise party for*... Gemma's birthday!

3 Complete the sentences below using the correct form of the verbs.

1 The conference .....*starts*..... *(start)* at 9 am, so we'll have to set off early.
2 It's very gloomy weather; I think I .*'ll stay*..... *(stay)* indoors today.
3 The only direct flight ...*leaves*....... *(leave)* at 5 am, which means an early start.
4 Sorry I'm late. I promise it *will not happ*.. *(happen)* again! *won't happen*
5 'Have you heard from Luca recently?' 'He *'s getting*...... *(get married)* next month.' *married*
6 Gwen and Tom .*are going* *(go)* to Mauritius for their honeymoon.
7 There's no hurry, the film .*doesn't*.. *(not / start)* until 9 pm. *start*
8 I normally leave work early on Friday, but this Friday I .*'m working*..*(work)* late.

will not = want

6

How do I form indirect questions?

1 Tick the correct sentence in each pair.

1 a   Can you tell me where is the bank?
  ✓ b   Can you tell me where the bank is?
2 a   He asked me what does 'kitsch' mean?
  ✓ b   He asked me what 'kitsch' means.

When we use a phrase like *do you know*, *can you tell* me, etc. in front of a question, the word order is inverted:

What does 'enigmatic' mean? → *Do you know **what 'enigmatic' means**?*

Where's the exam hall? → *Can you tell me **where the exam hall is**?*
When we report a question to someone else the same change in word order happens:
'What's the time?' → *He asked me **what the time was**.*

☆ Don't forget that in reported speech the verb goes back a tense.

2 Correct the mistake below.

He asked me what was my favourite band.

He *asked me what my favourite* band. *was*

3 Complete the sentences using the words in brackets.

1   Could you tell me *what time the next train is* (what time / next / train)?
✓ 2   I don't know *where the cinema is*. (where / cinema).
③   Could you tell me *if you came home* (you come home / late / tonight)? *are coming home*
④   They wondered *whether the film* (whether / film / start). *had started*
⑤   Have you any idea *how I get to* (how / I get to / Oxford Street)? *I get to*
✓ 6   She asked me *if I knew Ellen*. (I know / Ellen).
✓ 7   I asked her *what she wanted* (what / want / birthday). *for her birthday*
✓ 8   He wanted to know *when her birthday* (when / her birthday). *was*

TEST 1

1 Underline the most suitable tense.

1 When I _go / will go_ on holiday, I'll send you a postcard.

2 She asked me where _could she learn / she could learn_ Arabic.

3 If you _will get / get_ this new job, will you get a pay rise?

-ϸ (4) When _does the course finish / is the course finishing_?

5 I _go / am going_ to Oxford next week.

6 The plane _will arrive / arrives_ at 7 pm so we should make the connection.

7 Ring me as soon as _you get / you'll get_ here.

8 Annie _comes / is coming_ over this weekend.

2 Look at Emma's diary and complete the conversations using the correct form of the verbs in the box.

be	be
do	do
go	go
go	go
finish	leave
leave	meet
play	take

May

Thursday 7	1 pm – tennis
	7 pm – concert
Friday 8	2.30 pm – job interview!
Saturday 9	7 am – flight

Monica: Would you like to come for lunch on Thursday?

Emma: Sorry, I can't. I (1) am playing tennis.

Monica: What about dinner on Thursday evening?

Emma: I (2) am going to a concert.

Monica: When (3) will be _is_ your job interview? } timetabled event

Emma: It (4) is beeing _is_ on Friday afternoon.

Monica: Ring me as soon as it (5) finishs . What (6) are you doing (you) afterwards? will you do

-ϸ Emma: I don't know yet. I think I (7) will go am going straight home.

Monica: I (8) am meeting Julian at seven o'clock – why don't you come along and join us?

* * * *

Jamie: What (9) are yo doing (you) next weekend?

Emma: I (10) Im going to to Naples.

-ϸ Jamie: What time (11) you are leaving (you)?

Emma: Very early. The plane (12) leaves at 7 am.

-ϸ Jamie: (13) Will you go (you) to the airport by train? Are you going

Emma: I haven't thought about that yet. I think I (14) will take a taxi.

8

3 Emma rings the travel agent to ask some questions. Look at the advert and her notes, then complete her questions.

Tourwise Travel

Weekend in Naples

- Evening/morning flights
- Choice of 3* hotels
- Conveniently situated
- Day trips to Capri

1 How many nights is it?
2 Are the trips included in the price?
3 Do all rooms have showers?
4 How far is it from the station?
5 Can we visit Pompeii?

1 Could you tell me _how many nights_ it is?
2 Do you know _whether the trips_ includes are included in the price
3 Have you any idea _if all the rooms_ ? have showers
4 Do you have any idea _how far it is_ ? from the station
5 Can you tell me _if we can visit_ Pompeii?
   whether

4 Emma is back from holiday. Complete her friends' questions using the words in brackets. Use between two and five words.

1 'Is your Italian better now?' asked Peter. (*her*)
   Peter asked Emma if _her italian_ was better than
2 'What is Capri like?' asked Mariam. (*was*)
   Mariam asked Emma _what Capri was_ like.
3 'Do you have a suntan?' asked Anne. (*had*)
   Anne asked Emma _if she had_ a suntan.
4 'What do you think of Italian food?' asked Glenn. (*thought*)
   Glenn asked Anne _what she thought_ of Italian food.
5 'Do you want to visit Italy again?' asked Julia. (*wanted*)
   Julia wondered if Emma _wanted to visit_ Italy again.

5 Are these sentences right or wrong? Correct those which are wrong.

1 When will you get back from Italy? _When are you getting back from Italy?_
2 I'm not sure where is the exhibition. _I'm not sure where the exhibition is_
3 They asked me if my sister still lived in New York. _√_
4 I'll have a shower as soon as I'll get home. _as soon as I get home_
5 He wondered what did I do in my spare time. _what I did in my spare time_
6 Excuse me! Could you tell me where is the town hall? _where the town hall is_
7 She asked me why I was so late. _____
8 As soon as you'll come we'll have lunch. _As soon as you came, we'll have lunch._

9

4 Have or have got?

1 Tick the correct sentence in each pair.

1 a I'd got a terrible headache all day yesterday.
  (b) I had a terrible headache all day yesterday.
2 (a) I hope you have fun on the sailing course next week.
  b I hope you have got fun on the sailing course next week.

We can use either *have* or *have got* to talk about
owning or possessing something, or to describe
personal characteristics:
She's got a bad temper. = She has a bad temper.
We have a new car. = We've got a new car.

We use *have*, not *have got*, to talk about actions or experiences in expressions such as
have lunch, have a bath, have difficulty, have fun, have an accident, have a holiday, etc.
We don't usually <u>use *have got*</u> in the past or the future.
I usually have fun when I see Marcus. (Not ~~I usually have got fun~~ ...)
I had a pet rabbit when I was young. (Not ~~I had got a pet rabbit~~ ...)

2 Correct the mistake below.

> I've often got difficulty
> with phrasal verbs.

I ...*'ve often had difficulty*... with phrasal verbs.

3 Complete the sentences with the correct form of *have* or *have got*.

1 ......*Did you have*......... *(you)* a good holiday last week?
2 What time *does she usually* [have] *(she / usually)* lunch?
3 Mahmoud ...*has / has got*....... his own business in London, but he's hardly
  ever there. [don't have]
4 I'll have to do some overtime. I ...*haven't got*......... any money at the moment.
5 He can't walk very well at the moment, he ...*had*............... an accident
  last week.
6 My sister ....*had*............... very long hair when she was young.
7 Her new boyfriend ...*hasn't got*......... a very good sense of humour. He never
  gets a joke. [doesn't have]
8 'The reception on this line's not very good, what are you doing?'
  'I ...*'m having*......... a bath!'

do have = have got

10

When do I use the present perfect?

1 Tick the best sentence in each pair.

1 (a) That writer won a prize last year for his new novel.
  b That writer's won a prize last year for his new novel.

2 (a) Regina's been a secretary since 1999, even though she finds it very dull.
  b Regina is a secretary since 1999, even though she finds it very dull.

We use the present perfect:

- to talk about events that are relevant now or happened recently:
  Where's my mobile? **It's disappeared!**

- to refer to something that happened at some time in our lives, when the time is not important and not stated:
  I've met one of South America's most famous writers.

- to talk about something that started in the past and continues now (often with *for* or *since* to show how long):
  I've worked in London for five years. (I work there now.)
  I've lived in that flat since 1998. (I live there now.)
  (not ~~I live in that flat since 1998.~~)

We use the past simple to talk about events in the past or if we refer to a finished time:
I worked in London for five years but now I work in Sydney.

2 **Correct the mistake below.**

Have you ever been to Prague?

Yes, I've been there when I was a student.

Yes, I <u>went there when I was</u> .... a student.

3 Are these sentences right or wrong? Correct those which are wrong.

1 It's our anniversary. We ~~are married~~ for ten years. <u>We have been married</u>

✓ 2 This is the fourth time I've called but there's still no reply. ....

✓ 3 There's no milk left; someone's drunk it all. ....

✓ 4 I ~~have~~ worked as a translator when I lived in Spain. <u>I worked</u>

✓ 5 Where's John? I haven't seen him ~~since ages~~. <u>for ages</u>

6 I ~~never ate~~ Japanese food before, so I'd be curious to try it. <u>I have never eaten</u>

7 How many times ~~did you turn up~~ late for work last month? <u>have you turned up</u>

? 8 How many plays has Shakespeare ~~written~~? <u>did Shakespeare write?</u>

/ use of to do in Questions /

11

6 When do I use the past perfect?

1 Tick the correct sentence in each pair.

1 ✓a Sarah looked different because she had lost weight.
  b Sarah looked different because she lost weight.
2 ✓a I'd worked for five years by the time I started college last year.
  b I'd worked for five years by the time I'd started college last year.

We use the past perfect when we talk about the past and we want to refer to something that happened before this: *(present → past perfect)*
*By the time the fire brigade **arrived**, the building **had burnt down**.*
*The dog **ran** down the street. It **had jumped** out of the car.*
☆ Notice how we often use the past perfect and the past simple together.

We often use the past perfect after a reporting verb in the past:
*David asked me if Sarah **had lost** weight.*

We often use the past perfect when we talk about past events out of sequence. To talk about events in the same order as they happened, we use the past simple:
*The dog **jumped** out of the car. It **ran** down the street.* (after jumping out of the car)

2 Correct the mistake below.

> Two years ago I had
> been to Greece.
> I had sailed around
> the islands.

Two years ago ...*I went to Greece.   I sailed*... around the islands.

3 Complete the sentences using the correct form of the verbs.

1 She asked me if I ...*had seen*... (*see*) her cat.
2 When Paul started university he ...*had never lived*... (*never live*) away from home before.
-b 3 There's no point in going now! We ...*have missed*... (*miss*) the start of the film.
4 We arrived at the party at midnight, but most people ...*had left*... (*leave*) by then.
5 I was held up at work, so by the time I ...*arrived*... (*arrive*), they ...*had stopped*... (*stop*) serving hot food.
6 Typical! Just as I got into the bath the telephone ...*rang*... (*ring*)!
7 When she got home she ...*realised*... (*realise*) she ...*had forgotten*... (*forget*) her keys.
8 Why didn't you tell me you ...*had changed*... (*change*) your telephone number?

1 Underline the correct words.

1 Take some vitamin tablets! That's the second time you've come down with a cold *last month* / <u>*this month*</u>.

2 What's George been up to? I haven't heard from him since <u>*last week*</u> / *this week*.

3 John and Isobel fell out twice <u>*last month*</u> / *this month*.

4 We lived in Istanbul <u>*three years ago*</u> / *since 1998*.

5 She's really pestering him! That's the third time she's called him *yesterday* / <u>*so far today*</u>.

2 Read John's CV and the interviewer's notes. Write the interviewer's questions.

Curriculum Vitae

John Armstrong

Present	City & Co Solicitors
1994	Beacon & Sons solicitors, Beijing
1990	Leeds University: degree course

1 which school?
2 driving licence?
3 how long / qualified solicitor?
4 ever work / media law / before?
5 how long / work / City & Co.?
6 go / China / before 1994?
7 what / study / university?
8 how long / degree course?

1 (To) Which school did you go? ?
2 Do you have a driving licence? ?
3 How long have you worked as a qualified solicitor? ?
4 Did you ever worked in media law before? ?
5 How long did you worked for City & Co.? ?
6 Have you ever been to China before 1994? ?
7 What did you study at university? ?
8 How long was your degree course? ?

Questions !!!!!

3 **Fill in the gaps using the appropriate tense.**

A surprise too far

When I (1) ...*left*... (leave) college in Dublin in 1980, I (2) ...*went*...
(go) to Madrid to work for a large manufacturing company. I
(3) ...*had never worked*... (never / work) abroad before and I (4) ...*didn't know*... (not /
know) anyone in Madrid, so I (5) ...*found*... (find) it a bit lonely at first.
One weekend I (6) ...*decided*... (decide) to get a 'last minute' flight to
Dublin for a surprise visit to my boyfriend. When I (7) ...*arrived*...
(arrive) at Dublin airport I (8) ...*phoned*... (phone) him but he
(9) ...*wasn't*... (not be) at home. His flatmate (10) ...*told*... (tell)
me that he (11) ...*had gone*... (go) away for the whole weekend.
I (12) ...*felt*... (feel) so disappointed. I (13) ...*hadn't told*... (not tell) him
that I was coming because I wanted it to be a surprise.
I (14) ...*stayed*... (stay) the weekend then (15) ...*went*... (go) back to
Madrid on Monday morning. When I got to my flat I (16) ...*found*...
(find) a note under the door. It was from my boyfriend. He
(17) ...*had come*... (come) to Madrid at the weekend to visit me as a
surprise! By the time I (18) ...*got*... (get) the note he (19) ...*had flown*...
(fly) back to Dublin.

4 **Underline the correct tense.**

1 Of course I can't go out! I broke / _'ve broken_ my leg.
2 Despite the bad reviews, I think it's the best show I'd / _'ve_ ever seen.
3 Katri _'s waited_ / waited outside for two hours until her boyfriend arrived.
4 In your advertisement, you had stated / _stated_ that all the rooms have showers.
5 Two years ago my sister and I had gone / _went_ on a package holiday to Spain.
   It was a complete disaster! We had a terrible time.
6 The course _started_ / has started two weeks ago, so you should be able to catch
   up easily.
7 He's an old friend. I know / _'ve known_ him for ages.
8 Yesterday morning I've been / _went_ to enrol on a computing course.

/ fly - flew - flown /

14

7 Must or have to?

1 Tick the correct sentence in each pair.

1 a I must to go to an interview tomorrow.
   (b) I have to go to an interview tomorrow.

2 **(a)** Fiona fractured her wrist and had to go to hospital last week.
   b Fiona fractured her wrist and must go to hospital last week.

We use *have to / must* + infinitive to say it is
necessary to do something:
*I **must go** to the hairdresser.*
*I **have to go** to school.*

Must is only used in the present. We use forms
of *have to* for all other tenses:
*The last train was at midnight, so he **had to** leave early.*
*We've missed the bus so we'll **have to** walk.*

We often use *have to* for rules or things that other people think are necessary:
*I **have to** lose weight.* (the doctor told me to)

We often use *must* when the sense of <u>obligation</u> comes from the speaker:
*I **must** go to the doctor.* (I don't feel well)

2 Correct the mistake below.

I must to do more exercise.

I ..*have to do more*.. exercise.

3 Complete the sentences with the correct form of *must* or *have to*. Use one word only.

1 If you want to go away next month, you'll ......*have*...... to start saving money.

2 I'm exhausted! I ...*had*...... to work every weekend last month.

3 I haven't seen you for ages! We ...*must*...... meet up soon.

4 I can't stand ...*having*..... to wait in long queues at the bank.

5 Fire regulations say you ...*must*...... leave the building immediately if you hear the
   fire alarm.

6 We *have*...... to buy the ticket before we get on the train.

7 She's ...*had*...... to cut down on her expenses since she lost her job last month.

8 We don't have a spare room, so you'll ...*have*........ to share this one.

must = obligation

8 Mustn't or don't have to?

1 Tick the correct sentence in each pair.

1 ✓a The performance starts at 8 pm so we don't have to be late.
  ⓑ The performance starts at 8 pm so we mustn't be late.
2 ✓ⓐ You mustn't tell anyone because it's a secret.
  b You don't have to tell anyone because it's a secret.

Mustn't is used to say that something is not allowed:
*You **mustn't** smoke in here.* (it's not allowed)
*We **mustn't** shout.* (the baby is asleep, we'll wake her up)

Don't have to is used to say that it is not necessary to do something:
*I'm on holiday! I **don't have to** work for two weeks.*
*We **don't have to** whisper.* (there's no one else here)

2 Correct the mistake below.

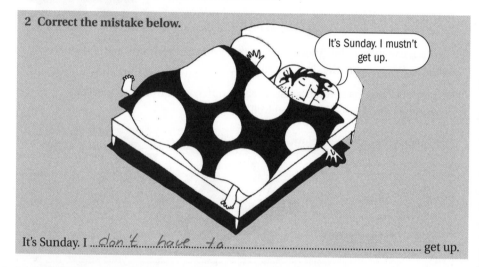

It's Sunday. I mustn't get up.

It's Sunday. I ...don't have to... get up.

3 Underline the correct words.

1 We <u>*don't have to*</u> / *mustn't* pay to get in. It's free.
2 Be quiet! You <u>*mustn't*</u> / *don't have to* talk in the library.
3 We *mustn't* / <u>*don't have to*</u> forget our tickets for the train, or we'll have to pay a fine.
4 <u>You *mustn't*</u> / *don't have to* wear a uniform. You can wear whatever you like.
→ 5 Tell Ahmed he <u>*mustn't*</u> / *doesn't have to* argue with his boss again, or he'll get the sack.
6 You <u>*don't have to*</u> / *mustn't* tidy your room. I tidied it this morning.
7 I *mustn't* / <u>*don't have to*</u> leave early. If I miss my bus I can walk home.
8 We <u>*mustn't*</u> / *don't have to* be late. They lock the doors after midnight.

16

Can, could, couldn't or be able to?

1 Tick the best sentence in each pair.

1 ✓a Eventually I could make her change her mind.
   ✓(b) Eventually I was able to make her change her mind.

2 a I'm worried that if I lose my job, I can't find another one.
   ✓(b) I'm worried that if I lose my job, I won't be able to find another one.

To say someone has the ability or possibility to do something in general, we usually use *can* (for the <u>present</u>) or *could* (for the <u>past</u>):
*I **could** run 10 miles a day when I was young.*

We can use *be able to* for all tenses:
*I **will be able to** run 10 miles a day if I practise enough.*

‖ To refer to a particular past situation, we use *was / were able to*. We don't use *could* ‖
‖ (but *couldn't* is possible):
*Even though the restaurant was crowded we **were able to** find a table.* (not ~~could find~~)
*We **weren't able to / couldn't** find a table because the restaurant was too crowded.*

We use *can* or *could* to ask for permission to do something, but not *be able to*:
***Can** I ask you a quick question?*

2 Correct the mistake below.

Am I able to borrow your suntan oil, please?

Conditional!

.....**Could   I   borrow**.. your suntan oil, please?

3 Are these sentences right or wrong? Correct those which are wrong.

1 Do you think I'm able to have a quick look at your newspaper? ....*could*...............

✓ 2 She couldn't find the suit you wanted. ....

3 When we went to Paris last month we ~~could~~ visit our mother. ...*were able to*......

➤ 4 My brother ~~can't~~ find a job <u>since</u> last May. *has not been able to find* !!!

5 Am I able to close the window? ...*Can I close*.... the window .

➤ 6 If you go to the sales next week you ~~are~~ probably able to pick up a bargain.
   you will probably able

➤ 7 I could play the piano when I was a child. ....*(not a situation)*

➤ 8 Unless you save some money, you can't afford the latest computer. *you wont be able*

| *could (polite ! Question !)* |
| *pefect: have / has been able to* |

TEST 3

1 Match the sentences 1–6 to those in a–f with the closest meaning.

1 You have to leave. ......*C*........   a You don't have to leave. ....

2 You don't have to stay. .....*d*........   b Can you stay? ....

3 You must stay. ......*f*........   c You mustn't stay. ....

4 Must you stay? .....*e*........   d You can leave. ....

5 You can stay. ......*a*........   e Do you have to stay? ....

6 Do you have to leave? .....*b*........   f You can't leave. ....

2 Complete the following sentences.

1 My sister *could* sing very well when she was young.

→ 2 My boss *wasn't able* to get there on time so we had to start without her.

3 You *mustn't* forget to lock the door, or we'll get burgled. *mustn't*

→ 4 My cousin is so well off that he .... work. *doesn't have to*

5 We *don't have to* go out. We can stay at home, if you like.

→ 6 *Can* I leave early today, or do I *have to* stay?

→ 7 I'm sorry, I *couldn't* get through all the work. I'll finish it tomorrow.

3 Use the correct form of *must, have to, be able to* and *can* to complete the letter below.

Dear Mum,

Thanks for your letter. I'm fine so you
(1) *mustn't* worry about me! It's not good
for you!

I'm settling in at college very well now. I eat in the
canteen most days, so I (2) *don't have to* cook.
My room in the hall of residence is quite big,
although I (3) *have to* share it with another
girl, so I (4) *mustn't* be too messy!
My lectures are all in the morning, so I (5) *have to*
get up early. The only day I (6) *can* have
a lie-in is Sunday. I hope I (7) *can* see you
next weekend. Do you think you (8) *will be able* to
come down for the day? You (9) *can* get a
bus to Cambridge, without (10) *having to* change.
See you soon.
Love, Sara

4 Complete the second sentence so that it means the same as the first, using the words in brackets. Use between two and five words.

1 Taking mobile phones inside the court is forbidden. (*mustn't*)
You *mustn't take* mobile phones inside the court.

2 We can't travel abroad without taking a passport. (*take*)
To travel abroad we *have to take a* passport.

3 There were no tickets left. (*couldn't*)
I *couldn't get* the tickets because they had sold out.

4 It isn't necessary to complete an application form. (*have*)
You *don't have to complete* an application form.

5 Will it be possible for us to leave our bags at the hotel? (*able*)
Will we *be able to leave* our bags at the hotel?

6 Don't use the telephone without asking me first. (*must*)
You *must ask me* before you use the telephone.

7 He couldn't find the embassy. (*able*)
He *wasn't been able* find the embassy.

8 It's against company regulations to wear jeans to work. (*wear*)
You *mustn't wear jeans* to work.

5 You went on a day trip, but it was not what you expected. Look at the advert and your notes, and write sentences about the tour. Use the correct form of *have to, be able to, could* and *couldn't*.

Day trip to Bath
- Great chance to see the Roman Baths.
- Visit the art gallery - free entry.
- You must buy tickets for the museum in advance.
- Open air concert in park.
- Pottery exhibition. Plenty of tickets available.
- Visit palace gardens with gatekeeper's permission.
- Tours in three different languages.
- Return coach transport provided.

1 No! Roman Baths closed.
2 No! Paid to get in.
3 No! Wasn't necessary.
4 Cancelled due to rain.
5 No! Sold out.
6 Visited gardens - didn't need permission.
7 Only English - we didn't understand.
8 No! Told us to catch train home.

1 We *weren't able to see the Roman Bath becaus they were closed.* (see)
2 We *had to pay a entrance fee at the art gallery* (pay)
3 We *didn't have to buy tickets in advance* (buy)
4 They *had to cancel the open air concert* (cancel)
5 We *couldn't get tickets for the pottery exhibition* (get)
6 We *didn't have to ask for permission* (ask)
7 We *couldn't understand the tour guide.* (understand)
8 We *had to catch the train home.* (catch)

19

10 Say or tell?

1 Tick the correct sentence in each pair.

1. ⓐ I invited Miriam but she said she was busy.
   b I invited Miriam but she said me she was busy.
2. a She left without telling where she was going.
   ⓑ She left without telling me where she was going.

Tell is always followed by a direct personal object. We *tell* someone something:
I'm a film star.
*She **told me** she was a film star.*

Say is not followed by a direct personal object. We *say* something:
*She **said** she was a film star.*

If we use a personal object with *say*, we must use *to*. We *say* something *to* someone:
*She **said to me** that she was a film star.*

There are a few expressions where we can use *tell* without a personal object:
tell a lie; tell the truth; tell a joke; tell a story; tell the time

2 Correct the mistake below.

She said me she would be slightly late.

She ....*told me she would be*.. slightly late.

3 Complete the sentences using *say* or *tell*.

1. She .....*said*...... to me that she'd just been made redundant.
2. Why don't they ...*say*.......... something, instead of sitting there in silence?
3. Carl is always ...*telling*...... me how hard he works, but I don't believe him.
4. Don't take his word for it, he never ....*tells*...... the truth!
5. I overheard Emily ...*saying*..... her mother was ill.
6. If you'd wanted to go out, you should have ...*told*......... me.
7. She ...*says*....... she doesn't gossip but she ....*tells*...... her friends everything.
8. What's the point of giving your son a watch if he can't ...*tell*......... the time yet?

11 Make or do?

1 Tick the correct sentence in each pair.

1 (a) Keeping fit isn't easy unless you make an effort.
  b Keeping fit isn't easy unless you do an effort.
2 (a) Ahmed said he'd like to do a course in Excel.
  b Ahmed said he'd like to make a course in Excel.

As a general rule, if we talk about jobs and work, we use *do*:
*I **do** the shopping, the washing up, the housework, and I **do** a full-time job!*

If we talk about creating or building something we use *make*:
*I **made** that!*

Common expressions using *make* and *do*:
make *an appointment, the bed, a decision, an effort, an excuse, friends, fun of someone, a fuss, a mess, money, a noise, a phone call, a photocopy, a plan, progress, a promise, a suggestion, a trip*
do *your best, business, a course, exercise, someone a favour, homework, the shopping, sport, work*

2 Correct the mistake below.

I make a lot of exercise.

I .....*do a lot of*.. exercise.

3 Complete each sentence using the correct form of *make* or *do*.

1 We need to ......*make*...... a decision about which candidate should get the job.
2 He's used to ...*making*.... a lot of business trips.
3 She's given me so much homework to ....*do*.......... I'll never get through it.
4 You're doing very well! You've ...*made*....... very good progress.
5 If you practised more you wouldn't ...*make*..... so many mistakes!
6 Can you ......*do*........ me a favour and drop me off at the bank?
7 I've just tidied up! Who's ...*made*..... all this mess?
8 It's not easy ...*doing*...... business with him when he's so unreliable.

12 Find out, make up, bring up, grow up or take off?

1 Tick the correct sentence in each pair.

1 (a) She was brought up in a small town called Winchester.
  b She was grown up in a small town called Winchester.

2 (a) I was so exhausted I took off my clothes and went straight to bed.
  b I was so exhausted I took out my clothes and went straight to bed.

- *Find (something) out*: to learn something by making enquiries or studying:
  *After careful research, I **found out** that he had gone bankrupt.*

- *Make (something) up*: to invent something:
  *I didn't want to go to dinner with her, so I **made up** an excuse.*

- *Bring (someone) up*: to look after a child until he / she is an adult:
  *I **was brought up** by my grandparents in Japan.*

- *Grow up*: to grow from a child into an adult:
  *My mother **grew up** in a small town.*

- *Take (something) off* (1): to remove an item of clothing, or something you were wearing:
  ***Take off** your shoes when you come in the house.*

- *Take (something) off* (2): to deduct:
  *The total amount is £600 but you need to **take off** £150 for expenses.*

2 Correct the mistake below.

After driving for several hours we found out a beautiful beach.

After ~~driving~~ *driving for several hours we found* a beautiful beach.

3 Are the underlined words right or wrong? Correct those which are wrong.

1 I <u>grew</u> in a very big family. ......*grew up*......

2 I was <u>grown up</u> on a small farm in the country. ....*brought up*.......

✓ 3 That's not true! You're <u>making it up</u>! ....

4 Her salary is only £10,000 when you <u>take up</u> the tax. ...*take off*............

✓ 5 You'd better <u>take off</u> that wet coat before you freeze! ....

➡ 6 My daughter has <u>grown up</u> five centimetres this year. ...*grown*...............

7 I couldn't <u>find out</u> the hotel because I'd lost the directions. ...*find*...............

✓ 8 Despite searching for hours on the internet, I couldn't <u>find out</u> what his surname was. ....

TEST 4

1 Complete the second sentence so that it means the same as the first sentence, using the words in brackets. Use between <u>two and five</u> words.

1 'Telephone me after work,' Marcus said to Kerry. (*told*)
   ✓ Marcus ..*told kerry to telephone him* after work.

2 'I don't want to go,' Sonia said. (*said*)
   ✓ Sonia ..*said she didn't want to* go.

3 'I don't like Paris as much as Prague,' Maria said to Nick. (*told*)
   ✓ Maria ..*told Nick she didn't like* Paris as much as Prague.

4 Could you photocopy this letter again? (*another*)
   ✗ Could you ..*do another photocopy* this letter?   *make another photocopy*

5 Make sure you're quiet if you get home late. (*noise*)
   ✓ Don't ..*make any noise* if you get home late.

6 Can you ask somebody for his home telephone number? (*out*)
   ✗ Can ..*you get out his* home telephone number?   *find out his*

7 Can you try hard to get the work finished? (*effort*)
   ✗ Can you ..*make effort* to get the work finished?   *make an effort*

8 I'll do everything I can to get tickets. (*best*)
   ✓ I'll ..*do my best to* get tickets.

2 Are these sentences right or wrong? Correct those which are wrong.

1 Why don't you take a chance and <u>say her</u> how you feel? ....*tell her*
2 They <u>did such a noise</u> at the party that the neighbours called the police. ...*made such a noise*
3 Amit <u>did Sally a great favour</u> when he told her about the job. ....
4 The bill wasn't too expensive when you <u>took out</u> the 10% service charge. ..*took off*
5 To put everyone at ease, David decided to <u>tell a joke</u>. ....
6 We'd known John <u>for two years</u> before we found he was married. ...*found out* ✓
7 Students are always <u>doing mistakes</u> with phrasal verbs. ....*making mistakes*
8 We had to <u>take out</u> our shoes when we went in the temple. .....*take off*

3 Underline the correct verb.

1 He *did* / *made* his best, but he still failed the exam.
2 Paul's getting out of shape these days, he should *make* / *do* some exercise.
3 Write back to me to *say* / *tell* me if you are interested.
4 Valerie *says* / *tells* she needs a break so why doesn't she take some time off work?
5 He *made* / *did* a promise not to tell anyone, but I'm sure he won't keep it.
6 I don't want to *make* / *do* a fuss, but I'm not happy with the results.
7 Can you *find* / *find out* whether he's coming or not?
8 I *made* / *did* an appointment for a haircut but I'll have to cancel it.

to / make an effort /   to do a favour
to / make a photocopy /

23

4 Complete the sentences using phrasal verbs with *bring, find, grow, make* and *take*.

1 If I *take off* my glasses, I wouldn't be able to read that sign over there.
2 Ben's parents died when he was quite young so he was *brought up* by his aunt.
3 Zoe has *grown up* so quickly that she's already into things like make-up.
4 I have to *find out* what the chemical formula for sulphuric acid is.
5 I asked him where he'd been, and he *made up* some excuse about meeting a friend at the airport.
6 Don't forget to *take off* £200 tax from the final amount.
7 Did you *find out* where the company is moving to?
8 I think Alex is *making up* that ridiculous story about meeting the President.

5 Complete the text below with **one or two suitable words** in each space.

I was (1) *telling* my friend Sara that I had booked a flight to Malta for the following week, when she (2) *told / said to* me that she had just bought a new car. I decided to ask her to (3) *do* me a favour and give me a lift to the airport.

She (4) *said* she would pick me up at 3 pm. At 4 pm she still hadn't arrived. I rang her house, and after speaking to her mother I (5) *found out* that she had gone out with her boyfriend instead. I (6) *did* my best to get to the airport in time, but I missed the plane. Afterwards she (7) *made up* a feeble excuse, and apologised.

I eventually made up with her, but only after (8) *making* the decision never to trust her again.

24

Like or as?

1 Tick the correct sentence in each pair.

1 (a) 'We've got a new teacher.' 'Oh, what's she like?'   *description*
　✓b 'We've got a new teacher.' 'Oh, how is she?'

2 ✓a 'What do you want to eat?' 'I'll have the same like you.'
　(b) 'What do you want to eat?' 'I'll have the same as you.'   *comparison*

We use *like*:
- to ask for descriptions or information about something or someone:
  'What's she like?' 'She's very kind and patient.'
- to say that something is similar or the same:
  *She looks **like Marilyn Monroe**.*
- to give an example:
  *Some names, **like Pat or Alex**, can be used for boys and girls.*

We use *as*:
- to make comparisons:
  *He's not **as tall as** his brother.*
- to describe a job or role:
  *She's working **as a web designer** at the moment.* (she is a web designer)

Compare:
*I work **as a psychologist**.* (I am a psychologist)
***Like** a teacher, I work with all sorts of people.* (my job is similar to a teacher's job)

2 Correct the mistake below.

Her hair is not as long like mine!

Her hair ....*is not as long as*.. mine.

3 Complete the sentences using *like* or *as*.

1 What's the new Chief Executive ....*like*.......?
2 Their house is very big. It's ....*like*...... a palace.   (*description, example*)
3 He's not .....*as*......... clever as you.   (*comparison*)
4 Your perfume smells ....*like*...... insect repellent!   (*description, example*)
5 She's working ....*as*......... a trainee consultant at the moment.   (*job*)
6 He's single, ...*like*...... most of his friends.   ↪ *Similarity*
7 She's very ....*like*....... her mother. They're both kind and easy-going.   *Comparison Similarity*
8 I wish I had a figure .....*like*..... yours!   *Similarity*

14 Which common nouns are uncountable?

1 Tick the correct sentence in each pair.

1 ✓ a He gave me a good advice about travelling round Egypt.
   ⓑ He gave me <u>some good advice</u> about travelling round Egypt.
2 ✓ a I would like an information about the latest laptop.
   ⓑ I would like <u>some information</u> about the latest laptop.

If a noun is uncountable, it has <u>no plural form</u>, and we <u>cannot use it with</u> *a / an:* ❓
*Where can I put all this **stuff**?*
*He bought new **furniture** for his flat.*
***Information** is easy to find on the Internet.*

Other common uncountable nouns include the following:
*accommodation, advice, damage, equipment, luggage, knowledge, news, research,
scenery, software, stuff, transport, work, weather*

We can use ***some*** with uncountable nouns. To refer to a specific amount we can use
words such as *a piece* of or *a bit of* in front of an uncountable noun:
***a piece of** equipment, **a bit of** advice*

☆ Some nouns can be <u>both countable and uncountable</u>, with different meanings:
*I had **a few** bad **experiences** on holiday last year.* (countable)
*The job requires someone with **experience**.* (uncountable)

2 Correct the mistake below.

I have a lot of luggages.

I have .....*a lot of luggage*... .

3 Are these sentences right or wrong? Correct those which are wrong.

1 That's ~~a~~ very good news. *That's very good news.*
2 He's at university doing ~~a~~ research on genetics. .....*research*....................
3 Let me give you ~~a~~ piece of advice. ....
4 He has two ~~works~~, one in the day and one in the evening. ....*two jobs*..........
5 Student ~~accommodations~~ are often cheap, but rather basic. .....*student accomodation*...
6 Where shall I put all ~~these~~ *this* equipment~~s~~? ....*Where shall I put all this equipment*.
7 She's bought ~~a~~ new software for her computer. .....*some new softwa*...
8 I never take much luggage. I always travel light. .....*?*.....*at*...........

26

Good or well?

1 **Tick the correct sentence in each pair.**

1　a　He plays in a band but he's not very well at singing.
　　ⓑ　He plays in a band but he's not very good at singing.
2　ⓐ　They mended the television and now it works as well as before.
　　b　They mended the television and now it works as good as before.

Good is an adjective and goes before the noun. *Well* is an adverb and comes after the verb. Compare:
*Isabel Allende is a **good writer**.*
*She **writes well**.*

*He's a **good artist**.*
*He **paints well**.*

We can sometimes use *well* as an adjective
to mean 'in good health':
*I'm not very **well**.*

We use *well* with a past participle for some expressions:
*He's very **well dressed**.*
*She's very **well known**.*

2 Correct the mistake below.

She plays football
good.

She ...*plays*....*football*....*well*........................... .

3 **Complete the sentences using *good* or *well*.**

1　He can ski, but he's not very ......*good*...... .
2　She can ski, but not very ...*well*......... .
3　Can I go home, please? I'm not feeling very ...*well*....... .
4　Their children are very ...*well*......... behaved.
5　He's a ...*good*...... singer. He sings extremely ...*well*......... .
6　I haven't eaten so ...*well*...... for years.
7　We had a very ...*good*...... time last night.
8　She's in an excellent job. It's very ...*well*...... paid.

27

1 Complete the answers using *good* or *well*.

1 How is she? She's very ...*well*........ .
2 What was the film like? It was very ...*good*...... .
3 Can he get by in Farsi? Yes, his Farsi is very ...*good*...... .
4 Does he speak good English? Yes, it's very ....*good*.... .
5 Can he cook? Yes, very ...*well*........ .
6 What was your meal like? It was very ...*good*........ .
7 Is he a good cook? Yes, he's very ...*good*........ .
8 How's your mother these days? She's very ...*well*........ .

2 Put a suitable word in each gap. In some sentences no word may be necessary.

1 I heard ....*an*.................... interesting piece of news yesterday.
2 Could I have your ticket? How much ....*luggage*............. do you have to check in?
3 I'd like some ....*information*........ about train times, please.
4 She's just been made redundant, so she's looking for a new ....*job*............ .
5 My stuff...........*is*................ in the cupboard. I'll move it later.
6 We're having ....— very bad weather for this time of year.
7 We need someone with ....— experience in public relations.
8 Could you give me ....*some*................../...... advice, please?

3 Underline the correct words.

1 I've ordered the same *like* / *as* I had last time.   *comparison*
2 Dishes with cream *as* / *like* spaghetti carbonara are quite fattening.
3 He wants a new computer *as* / *like* mine.
4 She's not as tall *like* / *as* her sister.
5 I'd like some *information* / *informations* on cinema times.
6 Cities *as* / *like* Oxford have got plenty of sights to see.
7 We've taken loads of photos of the amazing *sceneries* / *scenery*.
8 She's doing *some* / *a* research into the effects of global warming.

4 Complete the second sentence so it means the same as the first, using the words in bold. Use between two and five words.

1 Do you have any suggestions on where I should go? (*advice*)
    Could you give ~~me~~ *some advice* on where I should go?
2 'You're an excellent tennis player!' the coach told Tom. (*played*)
    The coach told Tom *he played very* well.
3 'Could you give me a description of your mother?' (*like*)
    'What does *your mother look*?' *like*
4 Denzil and his father are very similar in appearance. (*look*)
    Denzil ...*looks like*....... his father.

5 We're looking for someone who's worked in this field before. (*experience*)

└ We need someone _with experience_ in this field.

6 He's a very famous singer, lots of people have heard of him. (*well*)

→▷ He's a _well - known_ singer.

7 She's doing waitressing at the moment. (*as*)

She's working _as a waitress_ at the moment.

8 I'd like to find out about the course. (*information*)

I want to get _some information_ about the course.

5 Read the letter and Anish's notes, then write his questions below.

Dear Anish,

Here's the information I promised about Manchester University. It's not too far from London, and they have a very big campus. You can live on campus or nearby. They have all sorts of postgraduate courses. I am sure you'll find one you like. I know you're particularly interested in Human Rights, so I'll see if there's anything on their website.

I'll send my friend Charlie to meet you at the airport when you arrive. You met him a few years ago, but he's changed a lot since then. Both your aunt and I look forward to seeing you again.

See you soon,

Pat.

1 provide / accommodation?
2 advice?
3 facilities?
4 research / specialist field?
5 information / postgraduate courses?
6 website / like?
7 Manchester / big / London?
8 appearance / now?

1 Do they _provide students 'accomodation_

▷ 2 Can they _give me some advice on_ what to study?

▷ 3 What _kind of facilities they offer_? _are the facilities like?_

✓ 4 Can I _do research in a specialist_? _field_

▷ 5 Can they _give me some information about_? _on postgraduate courses_

6 What's _their website like_?

7 _Is_ Manchester _as London_?

→▷ 8 What does _he look like now_?

give sb some advice **on** st.

give sb. some information **on** st.

29

When do I use an apostrophe?

1 Tick the correct sentence in each pair.

1. (a) The hotel is quite small. Its maximum capacity is 40 guests.
   b. The hotel is quite small. It's maximum capacity is 40 guests.
2. (a) Whose books are these?
   b. Who's books are these?

We use an apostrophe:

- when we contract two words. The apostrophe goes in place of the omitted letters:
  they've = they have; it's = it is or it has; who's = who is or who has
- to show the possessive. We use *-'s* with singular nouns, irregular plurals and names:
  *the **man's** umbrella; the **children's** school; **Sonia's** book*
- For regular plural nouns that end in *-s* we put the apostrophe after the *-s*:
  *I can never remember my **students'** names.*

We don't use an apostrophe:

- with possessive forms such as *its, hers, his,* and *whose*:
  *The cat ate **its** food.*
- when we add *s* to a singular noun to make it a plural:
  drinks

2 Correct the mistake below.

Speech bubble: The dog's chasing it's tail.

The ...*dog's chasing its*... tail.

3 Add an apostrophe where necessary.

1. Where are the ladies shoes? ....*ladies'*...........
2. That dog just bit its owner. Its very vicious. ...*It's very vicious*
3. Whos got the key to the childrens room? .....*Who's got the key to the children's room*
4. They sell womens clothes and childrens shoes. *They sell women's clothes and* " *shoes*
5. Theyve just had a new baby. Its names William. ...*They've*............*Its name's Willie*
6. We dont like the room. Its too small and its heating system doesnt work. ..*We don't like the room. It's too*
7. Theres a kiosk selling drinks and pizzas nearby. ....
8. My best friends business closed three years ago. ...*friends'*...............

30

When do I use a capital letter and a comma?

1 Tick the correct sentence in each pair.

1 (a) He's a Buddhist monk from Thailand.
   b He's a buddhist monk from thailand.

2 a He's the new managing director.
   (b) He's the new Managing Director.

We use a capital letter:
- for languages and nationalities:
  French, Spanish
- For days and months, but not seasons:
  Monday, June, (but *summer*)
- For names or titles of people, places and things:
  Nelson Mandela, Edinburgh University

- For titles of books and films:
  Titanic, War and Peace
- For religions, festivals and holy days:
  Islam, Christmas, Easter

We use a comma:
- to separate words in a list (the final comma is optional):
  maths, chemistry, physics(,) and biology
- to separate long clauses in a sentence, particularly before *but, and, yet, while* and *or*:
  *I haven't found a dance class yet, **but** I'll carry on looking for a while.*
- after expressions at the beginning of a sentence like *of course, in my opinion, first of all*:
  First of all, *could I remind you that it was never my idea to go to Madrid!*

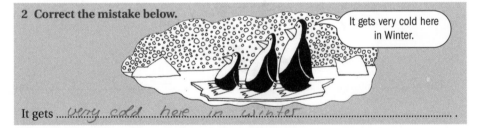

2 Correct the mistake below.

It gets very cold here in Winter.

It gets ...*very cold here in winter*... .

3 Add capital letters and / or commas where necessary.

1 They're going on a trip to the tower of london. ....*Tower of London*....

2 You could try renting through a letting agency,or you could contact the <u>landlord</u> direct.
....

3 I'm going home in December for Christmas and New Year. ....

4 That's Jack's new car. It's a range rover. ..*Jack*.... *Range Rover*

5 Chris has just been made the new chief executive. ...*Chief executive*

6 emma roberts bought a house,overlooking the thames. ..*Emma Roberts*.. *(Thames !)*

7 You haven't convinced me so far, but I can see what you're saying. ....

8 Jo's studying at Yale University,but none of her sisters went to university. ....

31

18

1 **Tick the correct sentence in each pair.**

1 (a) It was very embarrassing when I called him by the wrong name.

   b It was very embarassing when I called him by the wrong name.

2 a I'm writting with reference to your advertisment.

  (b) I'm writing with reference to your advertisement.

When a word ends in one vowel and one consonant, we usually double the final consonant before an *-ing, -ed, -er* and *-est* ending:

shop → *shop**ping*****   *run* → *run**ning*****   *big* → *big**ger***

For words with two or more syllables, in British English we double the final consonant if the final syllable is stressed, or if the word ends in *-l*:

prefer → *prefer**red*****   *travel* → *travel**led*****, *travel**ling***

☆ Note that American English retains the single consonant:

prefered, traveling

Be careful not to add an extra *-l* onto adjectives ending *-ful*: *beautiful, useful*, etc.

In British English, *practise* is the verb and *practice* is the noun. These words are frequently misspelt:

accommodation, advertisement, because, beginning, bicycle, centre, comfortable, definitely, different, disappointing, environment, grateful, really, which

2 Correct the mistake below.

> MANAGER

> Emma's pay increase was very dissapointing.

Emma's ...*pay increase was very disapointing*.......................... .

3 Underline the correct spelling of the words in italics.

1 *Which* / *Wich* is the correct spelling?

2 I'm looking for *accommodation* / *accomodation* in London.

3 We will *definitely* / *definitly* meet next week.

4 There are talks on protecting the *enviroment* / *environment*.

5 Hopefully we'll have a change of *government* / *goverment* after the next elections.

6 I would *realy* / *really* like to meet your parents one day.

7 They spent a couple of weeks in Bali and had a *wonderful* / *wonderfull* time.

8 Let's meet in the bar. It's more *comfortable* / *confortable*.

/disappointed , Cancelled, **32** accommodation /

1 Find ten spelling mistakes in this email and correct them.

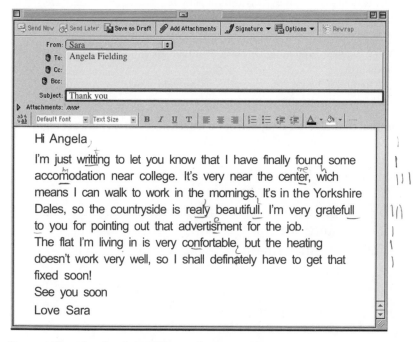

Hi Angela,

I'm just writting to let you know that I have finally found some accomodation near college. It's very near the center, wich means I can walk to work in the mornings. It's in the Yorkshire Dales, so the countryside is realy beautifull. I'm very grateful to you for pointing out that advertisment for the job.
The flat I'm living in is very confortable, but the heating doesn't work very well, so I shall definately have to get that fixed soon!
See you soon
Love Sara

2 Correct the mistakes in spelling and punctuation.

1 You need to consider peoples' feelings before you speak. ...*people's*...
2 I was realy dissappointed with my exam results. ...*really disappointed*
3 The student's names must all be written on the register. ...*students'*...
4 Even though, it's a very difficult course he'll probably pass. ...*it's*...
5 That's the oldest building in the area. It was built at least 800 years' ago. ...*years*...
6 I bought courgettes, aubergines, peppers, and tomatoes. ...
7 Every Summer we go to Brighton for a week in august. ...*summer August*
8 She couldn't make the appointment, so she canceled it. ...*cancelled*...

3 Insert an apostrophe where necessary.

1 My sisters name is Emily. ...*sister's*...
2 My sisters names are Estelle, Mireille and Valerie. ...*sisters'*...
3 It's such a beautiful day that we're going out to the park. ...
4 Lukes feet are so small that he has to buy childrens shoes. *Luke's children's*
5 Im afraid its not very good news about the exam. ...*it's I'm*...
6 The company closed its office in São Paulo two years ago. ...
7 At the moment Im writing a children's book, but I normally write for adults. *I'm*
8 It's a good film, but I cant remember its name. ...*It's*...

a children's book = kinderbuch

4 Complete the rest of the missing words.

1 I saw an *ad_vertise_m_ent* for the room in the newspaper.
2 When I move to Manchester I'll have to find some *ac_commodat_ion*.
3 The easiest way to get about in Amsterdam is by *b_icy_cle*.
4 Is everybody sitting *co_mforta_bly?*
5 I will *def_initel_y* come to your party, I promise!
6 We don't like the new Managing Director as much, we *pr_eferr_ed* the previous one.
7 Hurry up! The film is *be_ginni_ng right now!*
8 Their performance in the match last night was very *di_sappoint_ing.*

5 Insert a comma, capital letter or apostrophe where necessary. There are eight mistakes.

Most people believe that the pyramids in Egypt were built as tombs for the Pharaohs, but there are also a number of other theories. Some people believe, that the Great Pyramid was used to calculate the future, and that its already correctly predicted the First World War. Other people believe, its use was that of a giant calendar to measure the length of the year.

Each pyramid took roughly five years' to build. There are over 90 pyramids in Egypt, but its unlikely we'll ever find out, what the Ancient Egyptians really used them for.

I don't believe it – it's crashed!

Confusing nouns

1 Tick the correct sentence in each pair.

1 a We are destroying our nature with pollution.
  b ✓ We are destroying our environment with pollution.

2 a ✓ For a long journey it's easier to go by plane.
  b For a long travel it's easier to go by plane.

Nature, countryside or *environment*?

- *Nature* refers to all the things in the world that are **not made or caused by people** – **animals, plants, storms**, etc.
- *Countryside* refers to **land away from towns**, with fields and trees:
  *The **countryside** in Wales is beautiful.*
- *Environment* refers to the **natural world in which people, plants and animals live**.

Travel, journey, way or *trip*?

- *Travel* is used to describe the **general activity of moving** from one place to another:
  *The job involves a lot of **travel**.*
- *Journey* describes going from **one particular place to another**:
  *Did you have a good **journey**?*
- *Way* refers to a **route, a path, a direction** or a distance in space and time:
  *It's a long **way** from New York to Los Angeles.*
- *Trip* is used to talk about an **excursion or holiday** which is usually **for pleasure**:
  *We're going on a **trip** to the seaside next week.*

2 Correct the mistake below.

I love walking in the nature!

I love _walking in the countryside_ ....!

3 Underline the correct words.

1 I have a two hour *travel* / *journey* / *way* to work every morning.
2 People are moving from the *nature* / *countryside* / *environment* to the towns to look for work.
3 Unleaded petrol is better for the *nature* / *countryside* / *environment.*
4 I had a difficult *travel* / *journey* / *way* to work because of the train strike.
5 Brian went on a *journey* / *trip* / *travel* to France last month and had a great time.
6 The quickest *travel* / *journey* / *way* to my house is through the park.
7 Eva goes camping so she can be close to *nature* / *countryside* / *environment.*
8 Using aerosols is very harmful to the *nature* / *countryside* / *environment.*

35

20 Confusing adjectives

1 Tick the correct sentence in each pair.

1 a You can never feel boring in London.
  (b) You can never feel bored in London.

2 a I thought I'd be bored but my new job was great funny.
  (b) I thought I'd be bored but my new job was great fun.

Boring or *bored*?
- We use adjectives ending in *-ed* to show how we feel about something:
  I'm **interested** in geology. I'm **disappointed** with my exam results.
- We use adjectives ending in *-ing* to describe the thing which makes us feel this way:
  Geology is **interesting**. My exam results are **disappointing**.

Fun or *funny*?
- We use *fun* to describe something we enjoy doing:
  Ice-skating is **fun**.
- We use *funny* to describe something which makes us laugh, like a joke:
  John's very **funny**, he should be a comedian!

Nervous or *irritable*?
- We feel *nervous* when we are worried about something we are going to do (e.g. go on a plane, make a speech, start a new job, etc.):
  He's **nervous**. He's about to do an exam.
- We feel *irritable* when we get annoyed or angry easily:
  She's very **irritable** in the mornings.

2 Correct the mistake below.

Sam is very nervous when he's just woken up.

Sam is ..... *very irritable when he's just woken up*

3 Underline the correct word in each sentence.

1 I'm very *disappointing / <u>disappointed</u>* that I've failed my test again.
2 My boss has just given up smoking so she's really *<u>irritable</u> / nervous*.
3 It can get very *<u>boring</u> / bored* in a seaside town in winter.
4 The film was very *fun / <u>funny</u>* and cheered us all up.
5 I'm *surprising / <u>surprised</u>* at how many people were there.
6 He always gets *irritable / <u>nervous</u>* before he goes on a plane.
7 It was *fun / funny* when we all went out together. We should do it more often.
8 She's *interested / interesting* in doing a degree in French.

irritable = gereizt

nervous = nervös, etwas in tun

How do I use *get*?

1 Tick the best sentence in each pair.

1 a She knew Oliver while they were hiking round Scotland.
   (b) She got to know Oliver while they were hiking round Scotland.
2 a I need to take a ticket at the station.
   (b) I need to get a ticket at the station.

- *Get* can mean 'to obtain':
  *I need to **get** money from the bank.*

- *Take* means 'to carry something with you when you go somewhere':
  *Don't forget to **take** your phone with you.*

- *Get to* can mean 'to travel and arrive in a place':
  *It took me three hours to **get to** work today.*

- We use **go to refer** to the **mode of transport**, or to the **destination**:
  *I **go** to work by bus.*

- *Get to know* means 'to meet and find out about someone':
  *I **got to know** Sarah when we went on the training course.*

  After that you *know* him / her:
  *I've **known** Sarah for three months now.*

2 Correct the mistake below.

I need to go to the station in ten minutes! My train leaves at 1.30!

I need to ...*get to the train station in ten minutes*... at 1.30!

3 Underline the correct verb in each sentence.

1 I decided to *get* / *take* a ticket in advance as it was cheaper.
2 It's better to *get* / *go* to work by bicycle than by car.
3 They invited me to *get* / *go* to the new launch party next week.
4 There was a long traffic jam so it took me ages to *go* / *get* home.
5 You can *get* / *take* very good salads from that shop.
6 I'd like to *know* / *get to know* your sister sometime.
7 I'm just popping to the cashpoint because I need to *get* / *take* some cash.
8 If you're going on holiday make sure you *get* / *take* enough cash with you.

1 Underline the correct word in italics.

1 Halfway through the speech Anne began to feel very *boring* / *bored.*
2 Alex has a short temper and gets very *nervous* / *angry* when people push in a queue.
3 Let's all travel together as it will be more *fun* / *funny*.
4 He organises days out in the *countryside* / *nature*.
5 She felt very *embarrassed* / *embarrassing* when she tripped up in front of everyone.
6 We harm the *nature* / *environment* when we travel by car everywhere.
7 Your idea sounds very *interesting* / *interested* but I need more details.
8 Last night was *fun* / *funny* and we all enjoyed ourselves

2 Fill in the gaps with one suitable word.

(1) *I go* to work every day by tube. It takes me fifty minutes to (2) *get* there. The (3) *journey* is not an easy one since I have to change lines, but in fact it's not a long (4) *way* to drive if you (5) *go* by car. I have to make sure I set off before rush hour though, since long traffic jams in the morning can make me very (6) *irritable* by the time I arrive. Sometimes I wish I lived in the (7) *countryside* so I could walk to work without breathing in pollution. Walking to work, or cycling there, would be much more (8) *fun* than going by tube.

3 Complete the second sentence so that it means the same as the first, using the words in brackets. Use between two and five words.

1 He always makes us laugh a lot. (*have*)
→ We *always have fun* with him.
2 It's a four hour plane ride to Beirut. (*takes*)
→ It *takes four hours to get* to Beirut by plane.
3 The film she saw made her laugh a lot. (*film*)
She must have found *the film funny* as she laughed a lot.
4 While I was in Madrid I met a few people and we became friends. (*know*)
→ I *got to know a few* people while I was in Madrid.
5 It takes a long time to get to Delhi. (*is*)
The *journey to Delhi is* a long one.
6 The news that John was resigning was very surprising. (*hear*)
I was *surprised to hear* that John was resigning.

38

7 I <u>always</u> enjoy myself in his aerobics class. |(*have*)

I *have fun in his* aerobics class.

8 My exam results were disappointing. (*with*)

I *was disappointed with* my exam results.

4 Fill in the gaps with a suitable form of the words in the box.

bore	interest	disappoint	fun
bore	irritate	embarrass	surprise

Actress Alecca White remembers her schooldays

When I was at school I was always getting into trouble. One day I remember I was sitting in the library feeling (1) *bored* when my friend Sarah came up to me. 'Are you (2) *interested* in having a little (3) *fun*?' she asked. I agreed immediately. We tiptoed to a corner of the library where there was a wet sponge in the cleaner's bucket, and we balanced it on top of the door. As our teacher walked in, it fell at her feet. She looked so (4) *surprised*! She shouted at us in front of everyone. It was very (5) *embarrassing* 'Sarah and Alecca!' she shouted, 'I'm very (6) *disappointed* in you both!' She was very (7) *irritable* for the rest of the afternoon. We were both given a detention, but it had certainly livened up a (8) *boring* day at school!

5 Are these sentences right or wrong? Correct those which are wrong.

1 We decided ~~to take~~ first class tickets for the journey. *to get* .

2 The ~~travel~~ on the train was very relaxing. *The journey*

3 I always get ~~boring~~ in his classes. *bored*

4 I can drop off those CDs on my way back home. ....

5 She gets ~~irritable~~ when the plane takes off. *nervous*

6 Where can I ~~take~~ a phonecard? *get*

7 I have to do a lot of ~~travel~~ for work. ....

8 Going to an amusement park can be funny for all the family. *fun*

39

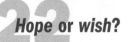

1 **Tick the correct sentence in each pair.**

1 a   The show was so funny. I wish you would be there.
   (b) The show was so funny. I wish you had been there.
2 (a) I hope you enjoyed your stay with us.
   b   I wish you enjoyed your stay with us.

We use *hope* and *wish* to say how we would like things to be.

We use *hope* for something we think is possible: *such past tense*
*I **hope** we **can** see you soon.* (we might see you)

We use *wish* + past tense for something which is unlikely / impossible:
*I **wish** we **could** come to London again.* (we can't come)

We use *wish* + past perfect when we express regret for something that happened in the past:
*I **wish** I **had seen** the job advert.* (I didn't see the job advert)

We use *wish* + *would* to say we don't like someone's current behaviour, and that we would like them to act differently:
*I **wish** you **would** let me know what you're thinking!* (you don't let me know)

2 Correct the mistake below.

I wish you have a wonderful time here!

I ...*hope you have* .... a wonderful time here!

3 **Fill in the sentences below with the correct form of *hope* or *wish* and the words in brackets.**

1   He's going to take an exam. ....*I hope he passes*......... *(he / pass)*
2   I *wish I had worked* *(I / work)* harder for the exam. I'm sure I've failed.
3   I *wish I could* .... *(I / come)* with you, but I'll be working all next week.
4   I *wish I didn't have* *(I / not have to)* work! Why is life so hard?
5   Good luck! We *hope you win* *(you / win)* first prize.
6   Milena comes back from holiday today. I *hope she enjoyed* *(she / enjoy)* it.
7   Be quiet! I *wish you would stop* *(you / stop)* whistling all the time!
8   She left work half an hour ago so I ...*hope she arrives* *(she / arrive)* in time for the performance.

40

How do I express an opinion?

1 Tick the correct sentence in each pair.

1 a The plan has some benefits but on the other side it has some problems.
 (b) The plan has some benefits but on the other hand it has some problems.
2 (a) In my opinion, buying an investment property can be risky.
 b According to me buying an investment property can be risky.

Use *on the one hand ... on the other hand* to introduce two different points of view:
On the one hand, cycling to work is good exercise. **On the other hand**, you breathe in a lot of fumes, which is bad for you.

To say the exact opposite of something is true, we use *on the contrary:*
Tea is not necessarily bad for you. **On the contrary**, it can be good for you.

To say what we think, we use *in my opinion:*
In my opinion, we shouldn't pay tax on clothes.

To state someone else's opinion, we can use *according to:*
According to John, nurses don't earn enough money.

Firstly and *first of all* are used to introduce our first point:
Firstly, I will explain my theory on the use of acupuncture to cure back pain.

At first describes the beginning of a situation, often with *but* if the situation changes:
At first, I didn't like her, but now I think she's quite nice.

2 Correct the mistake below.

Firstly, I didn't like eating snails but now I enjoy them.

At first I didn't like eating snails... but now I enjoy them.

3 Are these sentences right or wrong? Correct those which are wrong.

1 He's not mean. On the contrary, he's very generous. ....correct...........
2 If we move we can buy a bigger house. On the other hand, we'll lose touch with our friends.
....
3 Our objectives are ~~at first~~ to recover from last year's losses. ...firstly...............
4 ~~According to me,~~ we should get more public holidays. ..In...my...opinion.
5 A new terminal could be useful. ~~On the contrary,~~ it could be very noisy. On the other hand
6 Firstly, check the prices of the hotels, then book the cheapest. ......correct !!!......
7 According to Dr Su, animals shouldn't be kept in zoos. ....
8 Firstly, Karim was very shy, but he soon settled in. ....

According to sb

on the contrary

24 When do I use *in* and *to*?

1 Tick the correct sentence in each pair.

1   a   Could you explain us why you weren't at the meeting?

    ⓑ   Could you explain to us why you weren't at the meeting?

2   ⓐ   Abigail is taking a course in Arabic so she can get by in Syria.

    b   Abigail is taking a course on Arabic so she can get by in Syria.

- *In*

   We read something *in* a newspaper, or *in* an advertisement:
   *I read an article about windsurfing **in** the newspaper.*

   We take lessons *in* Spanish, or a course *in* Arabic:
   *Solange is taking an evening course **in** Excel to improve her job prospects.*

   We are interested *in* something:
   *I'm interested **in** Persian history.*

- *To*

   We *look forward to* something:
   *I **look forward to** hearing from you.*

   We *describe / explain* (something) *to* someone:
   *I'll **describe to** you how to get to the station.*

   We *write / speak / listen to* someone:
   *Naomi **wrote to** the shop the next day to ask for a refund.*

2 Correct the mistake below.

I saw the car on your advertisement.

I <u>Saw the car in yours</u> .... advertisement.

3 Complete the sentences with a preposition.

1   She's looking forward ....*to*......... starting her new job.

2   I read about the earthquake ......*in*.......... the newspaper.

3   He promised that he would write .....*to*.......... her every week.

4   I'm interested ......*in*.......... the special offer I saw ...*in*............ your advertisement.

5   I explained ......*to*......... Angela that she would have to send in a written application.

6   Amy's taking lessons .....*in*............ flamenco dancing so she can impress everyone.

7   Could you stop daydreaming and listen ......*to*.......... me please?

8   Can you describe .....*to*.......... me what she looks like so I'll recognise her?

TEST 8

1 Complete the second sentence so that it means the same as the first, using the words in brackets. Use between two and five words. 2-5

1 The first time I tried smoked salmon I wasn't keen on it. (*like*)
   At *first I didn't like* smoked salmon.

2 I don't think it's a good idea for you to go back to college. (*my*)
   In *my opinion, it's not* a good idea for you to go back to college.

3 Please stop asking so many questions! (*wish*)
   I *wish you wouldn't ask* so many questions!

4 He's very eager to see her again. (*forward*)
   He's *looking forward to seeing* her again.

5 I trust you enjoyed your evening. (*hope*)
   I *hope you had* a good time.

6 Before doing anything else, preheat the oven to 180 degrees. (*of*)
   First *of all, preheat the oven* to 180 degrees.

7 However, joining the EU could also have some disadvantages. (*other*)
   On *the other hand,* joining the EU could also have some disadvantages.

8 I should have worked harder at school! (*wish*)
   I *wish I worked* at school!   *past perfect !!*
   had harder

2 Are these sentences right or wrong? Correct those which are wrong.

1 I saw the course advertised in the newspaper. ....

2 He's taking a course ~~of~~ Spanish and French. ......*in*..........

3 The election results are ~~on~~ all the newspapers! ......*in*..........

4 We look forward to hearing from you soon. .....*correct !!!*

5 I've explained James that he needs to check with you first. .....*explained to*

6 We've booked a restaurant where we can ~~listen~~ jazz music. .....*listen to*

7 I saw a very cheap flight ~~on~~ that advertisement! .....*in*..........

8 I'm ~~looking forward~~ some peace and quiet when the kids go. .....*Lookin forward to*

3 Complete each sentence with an appropriate word.

1 First .....*of*....... all you need to finish your degree, then you can think about travelling around Thailand.

2 *According*...... to the notice, the station is closed tomorrow.

3 I .....*hope*............... Jonathon passes his driving test.

4 Tara is looking forward .....*to*............... starting her new job.

5 I .....*wish*............... my mother would stop calling me every day!

6 It's freezing! I .....*hope*............... our train arrives soon!

7 Tarik is very interested .....*in*............... modern art.

8 We .....*hope*............... you will be very happy in your new home.

43

4 Complete the letter with one appropriate word in each space.

Dear Sam,

I (1) ...*hope*... you are well. Thank you for the invitation to your wedding next month. I saw the announcement (2) ...*in*... the newspaper.

I (3) ...*wish*... I could come, but unfortunately I will be attending a course (4) ...*in*... public speaking that week. I explained (5) ...*to*... my manager that I would really benefit from it, especially since (6) *according* to him I need practice in giving presentations. I'm not looking forward (7) ...*to*... it!

Anyway, I (8) ...*hope*... you and Muriel will be very happy together!

Best wishes,

Andrew

5 Are the sentences in the flier right or wrong? Correct those which are wrong.

✓	Southsea Language Centre runs courses of English every summer.	1 ...*in*...
✓	You can see our adverts on all the newspapers.	2 ...*in*...
✓	According *to* our students, it's the best course in Southsea.	3 ....
✓	Many students write *to* us to say how much they enjoyed it.	4 ...*to*...
✓	Successfully passing the course is not difficult, *on* the contrary, it's easy with our excellent tuition!	5 ...*r*...
✓	**If you are interested in our courses, contact us on** **01354 225334**	6 ...*r*...
✓	**To apply for the course on July, you need to book now!**	7 ...*in*...
✓	We look forward *to* hearing from you very soon!	8 ...*to*...

25 Still, yet or already?

1 Tick the correct sentence in each pair.

1 a Jon's only just bought his new car and he's still bored with it.
   (b) Jon's only just bought his new car and he's already bored with it.
2 (a) It's very late. Hasn't the film finished yet?
   b It's very late. Hasn't the film finished already?

Still means something is continuing, usually later than expected:
*Are you **still** asleep? It's 3 pm!*

Already means something has happened sooner than expected:
*Nadine has **already** left. She didn't want to wait for you.*

Still and *already* go in the middle of the sentence. With one-word verbs, they go before the main verb, but after *be*. With multi-word verbs, they go after the first auxiliary verb:
*I **still** find this map confusing. I'm **already** lost!*
*I've **already** been seen by the doctor. I'm **still** feeling ill.*

If there is a negative verb, it goes after *still* but before *already*:
*I **still** haven't seen that film. I hope you **haven't already** seen it.*

Yet means we expect something to happen. It is used with questions and negatives, and goes at the end of a sentence:
*He hasn't woken up **yet**.*

2 Correct the mistake below.

I can remember yet when you were this high!

I ....Can..still....remember........................ when you were this high!

3 Add *still*, *yet* or *already* to the sentences in italics.

1 You don't need to do the washing up. *I've done it.* ...I've already done it...
2 Jo's been unemployed for a year. *He's looking for another job.* He's..still..looking
3 Karen didn't want to see the new Scorsese film. *She's seen it.* She's..already..seen it.
4 Susan's a very bright child. *She's only three but she can read.* ......can..already..read
5 Chris sent the work in last month. *No one's paid him for it.* yet.........................
6 *They're looking for a cure for cancer after years of research.* They are still looking
7 He was paid three days ago. *He's spent it!* ...He's..already..spent it.
8 My phone has been out of order for weeks! *No one's fixed it.* yet.........................

45

Wortstellung !!!!

26 Very, too or enough?

1 Tick the correct sentence in each pair.

1 a Tony's too nice, so you're bound to get on with him.
  (b) Tony's very nice, so you're bound to get on with him.
2 (a) The food looks delicious but I don't want to break my diet.
  b The food looks very delicious but I don't want to break my diet.

Very means 'a lot' or 'extremely'. It goes in front of adjectives and adverbs:
*I was **very surprised** to hear that Harry's getting married.*

We don't use *very* with strong adjectives such as *astonished, awful, enormous*, etc.:
*I was **astonished** to hear that Harry's getting married.*

Too means 'more than necessary'. It goes in front of adjectives and adverbs:
*These shoes are **too big**!*

We often say *too ... to do something*. Compare:
*John was **too tired to come** along with us to the party.* (he didn't come)
*Hania was **very tired** but she came to the party.*

Enough means 'sufficient'. It usually goes before a noun but after an adjective:
*I can't get in the car, there's not **enough room**.*
*That suitcase is not **big enough** for everything I'm taking.*

2 Correct the mistake below.

Don't worry! The exam will be too easy!

Don't worry! The exam ...*will be very easy*... !

3 Complete the sentences with *very, too* or *enough* and the word in brackets. Sometimes no extra word is needed.

1 The film starts ...*very late*... *(late),* around midnight.
2 We arrived ...*too late*... *(late)* to hear the beginning of the lecture.
3 Compared to Holland, Australia is ...*enormous*... *(enormous).*
4 Carl is ...*very strong*... *(strong)* but he won't be able to carry the bed.
5 That restaurant isn't ...*busy enough*... *(busy)* to make much profit.
6 Sara was ...*too*... *(embarrassed)* to make a fuss when her food arrived late.
7 You must see the new Iranian film. It's ...*fantastic*... *(fantastic)!*
8 Don't take ...*too much*... *(much)* or there won't be ...*enough*... *(food)* to go round.

46

1 Tick the correct sentence in each pair.

1　a　Most of people know about email these days.
　　(b)　Most people know about email these days.

2　a　The amount of holiday you get depends of your employer.
　　(b)　The amount of holiday you get depends on your employer.

We use *of* in expressions such as:

* *to be fond of*: I'm very **fond of** cats.
* *to have experience of*: I have no **experience of** sailing.
* *in spite of*: She managed to get to sleep **in spite of** the noise.

We don't use *of*:

* after *despite*: **Despite** the rain we still went on the picnic.
* between *most* + noun, when *most* is followed directly by the noun. Compare:
Most restaurants in London are expensive.
Most of the restaurants I went to were very good.

We use *on* in expressions such as:

* *to depend on someone / something*: Jim **depends on** me.
* *to be keen on someone / something*: I'm **keen on** fishing.

We don't use *on* before *last / next*: She starts school **next** Monday.

2 Correct the mistake below.

Despite of their bad behaviour Amy adores her nephews.

Despite ...*their bad behaviour*.. Amy adores her nephews.

3 Insert *on* or *of* where necessary.

1　We'll start lessons next Monday if you are free then. ....*correct*................

2　I'm not very ~~keen~~ spicy food; it gives me indigestion. ....*keen on*.......................

3　The camera can take good pictures but it ~~depends~~ the film you use. ...*depends on*............

4　Farah doesn't have much ~~experience~~ organising conferences. ...*experience of*....

✓ 5　Despite the train strike, most people still got to work. ....

✓ 6　My cousin moved to New York last July. ....

✓ 7　Most people in that village depend on tourism for a living. ....

8　Most my friends are students at the moment. ...*Most of*...................

47

TEST 9

1 **Are these sentences right or wrong? Correct those which are wrong.**

1 Dario was ~~very~~ astonished to learn he had won the scholarship. ...*astonished*...
2 They might cancel the flight. It ~~depends~~ of the weather. ....*depends on*....
✓ 3 I don't think there's enough funding available for hospitals. ....
4 Tanya's so hard up she doesn't have money enough to go out. ...*enough money*...
5 Anna was ~~too~~ tired, but she stayed until the end. ...*very*...
6 Most of staff in that hotel are very helpful. ...*Most of the staff*...
✓ 7 Most of the underground staff are on strike at the moment. ....
✓ 8 I left a message for her but she hasn't got back to me yet. ......*✓*......

2 **Complete the second sentence so that it means the same as the first, using the words in brackets. Use between <u>two and five</u> words.**

1 I spoke to you about this issue before. (*already*)
I have ...*already spoken to you*.... about this issue.
2 We're sorry, but your room isn't ready yet. (*still*)
We're sorry but ...*your room still*.... isn't ready.
⇒ 3 When we arrived there they had finished eating. (*got*)
By the time we ...*got in they had already*... eaten.   *got there*
4 It's midday but we still haven't had breakfast. (*yet*)
We ...*haven't had breakfast yet*... and it's nearly midday.
5 My boss will decide whether or not I get a promotion. (*depends*)
It ...*depends on my boss whether*... or not I get a promotion.
6 Even though it was very hot, Jeremy wore his jacket. (*despite*)
Jeremy ...*wore his jacket despite*... the heat.
7 Nearly everyone puts on weight as they get older. (*most*)
As they get older ...*most people put*... on weight.
8 I wanted to go away last year but I had too little time. (*enough*)
I didn't ...*have enough time to*... go away last year.

3 **Fill in the gaps in the telephone conversation with one suitable word. Sometimes no extra word is needed.**

Carla: Hi Ben! Are you (1) ...*still*... travelling? Where are you calling from? Have you got back home (2) ...~~already~~...? *yet*
Ben: No, I'm in Thailand at the moment.
Carla: What! You're (3) ...*still*... there? You've been there for months! What about Tom?
Ben: He's (4) ...*already*... gone back home. He ran out of money. I might come back soon but it depends (5) ...*on*... my finances. Most (6) ...—... places here are very cheap, and I want to travel south. The people are (7) ...*very*... friendly, the food's (8) ...—... delicious, in fact I don't feel like coming back at all!

4 Insert a suitable word in the gaps. Sometimes no word is needed.

1 I've *already* seen that film, so I don't want to see it again.
2 I'd lend you my book, but I haven't finished it *yet* .
3 Most *——* people who live there speak at least some English.
4 Sarah's not very keen *on* the idea of moving to Manila.
5 John sang *very* badly but everyone still applauded him.
6 I've been waiting for ages and you're *still* not ready!
7 Don't forget, Jennifer's birthday is *——* next Sunday.
8 Despite *——* the fact she spoke no Greek, Emma found her way around easily.

5 James Borg is an actor who has just starred in a film. He is being interviewed for a teenage magazine. Write his answers.

1 In your film you play a footballer. Are you a sports fan?
(like / cricket / but / not fond / football)
I like cricket but I'm not fond of football

2 Do you have to be a football fan to enjoy your film?
(no / think / most / people / like)
No, I don't think so. Most people enjoy my film

3 Have you ever acted before?
(never / had / previous / experience / acting)
I never had a previous experience of acting in a film

4 What's it like?
(despite / long / hours / enjoy)
Despit long hours of working I enjoy it

5 Are you going out with anyone at the moment?
(no / not / enough / time / for girlfriend!)
No, I haven't enough time for a gilfrien

6 Will you be making a second film?
(we / already / started / sequel)
We alreade statet with the fired sequel

7 How are your friends coping with your new-found fame?
(most / my friends / very happy / me)

8 Do you think you'll carry on with a film career?
(depend / the success / this film)

28 When do I use *take*?

1 Tick the correct sentence in each pair.

1 a This rug is so filthy I'll have to take it to the cleaners.
  b This rug is so filthy I'll have to bring it to the cleaners.
2 a You should profit from the free bus rides.
  b You should take advantage of the free bus rides.

Take means to move something to a place away from the speaker.
*I'm **taking** some flowers to Michelle's house.*

Bring means to move something to the place where the speaker is.
*Can you **bring** some flowers when you come?*

We *take* a photograph / an exam / a break.
To *take advantage of* something means to make use of it.
To *profit from* or *benefit from* something means to gain from something.
To *take care of* means to look after someone or something:
*I'll have to **take care of** my parents when they get older.*

To *pay attention to* means to concentrate on something or someone.
*Make sure you **pay attention to** the instructions I send you!*

2 Correct the mistake below.

Can you ...*take a photo*... of us?

3 Complete the sentences with a suitable verb.

1 Adrian ...*takes care of*... all his grandfather's financial affairs now.
2 Can you ...*take*... my jacket to the launderette when you go?
3 Next time you come here to visit, *you should bring*... your parents with you.
4 Sara sunbathes too much. She should ...*take care of*... her skin.
5 Let's ...*take advantage of*... the cheap deals and go away somewhere.
6 Let's ...*take*... a break, I can't concentrate any longer.
7 Joanne never ...*pays attention*... to me when I give her instructions.
8 We should ...*benefit from*... that investment in a few years.

28 When do I use *the*?

1 Tick the correct sentence in each pair.

1 a I'm very grateful for information you sent.
   b I'm very grateful for the information you sent.
2 **a** Jessica spends most mornings watching television.
   b Jessica spends most mornings watching the television.

We usually use *the* to talk about a particular thing / person, when the speaker and listener know which ones we are referring to:
*I can't find **the CDs** which you lent me.* (we both know I am referring to particular CDs)

We don't usually use *the*:
- to talk about people / things in general:
  *It's often cheaper to buy **CDs** on the Internet.* (any / all CDs – not particular CDs)
- for countries, mountains or seas, unless it is a group of states or islands:
  *Lake Como, Mount Everest, Chile, **the** Bahamas, **the** United States*
- with meals:
  *have **breakfast**; eat **lunch**; finish **dinner***
- with certain common daily routines:
  go to work / school; be at home; be at work / school; go by bus / car; go home; watch TV

We use *a / an* to refer to something for the first time, and *the* to refer to it again.

Compare:
*I saw **a** lovely dress in the sales yesterday.*
***The** dress I bought yesterday was a bargain.*

2 Correct the mistake below.

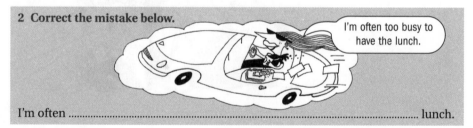

I'm often too busy to have the lunch.

I'm often .... lunch.

3 Insert *the* where necessary.

1 There's a sign saying we're not allowed to feed animals. ....the animals.........
2 I find that music really relaxes me after a day at work. ....
3 Lots of species become extinct as a result of pollution. ....
4 I spend most of my time at work doing research. ....
5 There was an oil leak and lots of fish died as a result of pollution. ....
6 Stella's neighbours had a party and music kept her awake. ....
7 My sister loves animals and she's training to be a vet. ....
8 Work that Jon does as a builder is very physically tiring. ....

30 Which verbs need an object?

1 Tick the correct sentence in each pair.

1 a   I hate it when people jump the queue.

   b   I hate when people jump the queue.

2 a   Tom couldn't believe when they told him he'd won first prize.

   b   Tom couldn't believe it when they told him he'd won first prize.

Some verbs need an object to complete their meaning:

- *enjoy* something:
  He really **enjoyed the latest James Bond film** in spite of the unrealistic plot.
- *appreciate* something:
  I would **appreciate it** if you would cancel my subscription.
- *find* something *interesting / difficult / useful*:
  I'd **find it very useful** if you could go over those figures again.
  ☆ Note the object comes between *find* and *useful*.
- *can't stand / can't bear* something:
  Jim **can't stand his neighbour** playing the trumpet.
- *love / like / hate* something:
  My father was brought up in a small town in Egypt and he still **loves it** there.
- *regret / prefer / need* something:
  Health services should be targeted at people who **need them**.

2 Correct the mistake below.

As soon as Ryan sent the joke email to his boss he regretted.

As soon as Ryan ....

3 Insert *it* where necessary.

1 I find difficult to believe that Ray would make a good teacher. ......*find it difficult*......

2 Emma really enjoyed herself at the party yesterday. ....

3 I can't stand when people turn up late for appointments. ....

4 Jamie can't stand people being hypocritical. ....

5 I spent £100 on the meal but I don't regret at all. ....

6 She told me she'd got a new job but I don't believe. ....

7 I'd prefer if you make an appointment before coming round. ....

8 Nadia regrets moving to the suburbs, and she misses the town. ....

1 Underline the correct word(s) in italics.

1 *Kindness / The kindness* is an essential quality in a friend.
2 We agreed to meet up and have *lunch / a lunch* soon.
3 Anthony has to be at *the work / work* by 6 o'clock every morning.
4 There's a factory next door and my car is filthy from *the pollution / pollution*.
5 A lot of couples argue about *the money / money*.
6 My purse was still there but all *the money / money* was gone.
7 *Unemployment / The unemployment* levels are getting worse.
8 You can look for visa information on *Internet / the Internet*.

2 Is each line in the letter below right or wrong? Correct those which are wrong. Sometimes there is a word missing, a wrong word or a word which is not needed.

Last month I decided to make a break, and wanted to
take advantage from the cheap flights that you can find
these days on Internet. I asked the travel agents for
advice on where to go, and since I love the history
they recommended visiting China. The climate was
perfect as I can't bear when it's too hot. There was so
much to see I knew I'd enjoy. However, I couldn't book
it as I had to take the visa by the next day!

1 ....
2 ....
3 ....
4 ....
5 ....
6 ....
7 ....
8 ....

3 Are these sentences right or wrong? Correct those which are wrong.

1 Annie wanted to benefit from the gym, since it was free. ....
2 If we get there at sunset we can make some good photos. ....
3 When you drive you need to take care of the road signs. ....
4 When I was young, my parents used to bring me to the zoo. ....
5 Tony tried to intervene but no one paid any attention for him. ....
6 Some people profited from the recession by buying property at low prices and selling later on. ....
7 As a student, you should enjoy advantage of the discount air fares. ....
8 If you keep a pet you must take care for it. ....

4 Fill in the gaps with an appropriate word. Sometimes no word is needed.

Too good to be true?

Liz Hardy tells of her lucky escape from a 'get rich quick' scheme.

A few months ago I was sent some information about
(1) .... tax-free investments. Apparently there was a new
tax-free scheme we could take (2) .... of, which would
double your money. I called the company and they assured me it was easy
to make a (3) .... with this scheme, and that they would
take care (4) .... everything, but I didn't believe
(5) .... I found (6) .... difficult to see
how this scheme would work. It just sounded too good to be true. An
adviser assured me that he would come to my house and
(7) .... all the documents with him so I could see for
myself. He came round but I wasn't at (8) .... home that
day. It was lucky I didn't join the scheme because a week later they went
bankrupt!

5 Complete the second sentence so that it means the same as the first, using the
words in brackets. Use between two and five words.

1 Janet feeds my cat whenever I go away. (*care*)
Janet .... my cat whenever I go away.

2 Listen carefully to everything the doctor says. (*pay*)
Make sure you .... what the doctor says.

3 I hate it when people have arguments about politics. (*stand*)
I .... people argue about politics.

4 I'd be grateful if we could have a room with a sea view. (*appreciate*)
I .... we could have a room with a sea view.

5 I still have problems with Arabic despite learning it for years. (*find*)
I've been learning Arabic for years but .... difficult.

6 I thought the film was very enjoyable even though it had been given bad reviews.
(*enjoyed*)
Despite the bad reviews the film had been given, I .... anyway.

7 Deepak is fascinated by archaeology and wants to study it. (*finds*)
Deepak .... and wants to study it.

8 I wish I hadn't left university without finishing my degree. (*regret*)
I left university without finishing my degree and .... now.

Answer key

Unit 1

1 1 a
   2 a

2 I'll be surprised if she passes her exams.

3 2 you have
   3 arrive
   4 gets
   5 finish
   6 arrives
   7 are
   8 will have to retake; fail

Unit 2

1 1 a
   2 a

2 Tonight we're having a surprise party for Gemma's birthday.

3 2 'll stay
   3 leaves
   4 won't happen
   5 's getting married
   6 are going
   7 doesn't start
   8 'm working

Unit 3

1 1 b
   2 b

2 He asked me what my favourite band was.

3 2 where the cinema is
   3 if you are coming home late tonight
   4 whether the film had started
   5 how I get to Oxford Street
   6 if I knew Ellen
   7 what she wanted for her birthday
   8 when her birthday was

Test 1

1 1 go
   2 she could learn
   3 get
   4 does the course finish
   5 am going

   6 arrives
   7 you get
   8 is coming

2 1 'm playing
   2 'm going
   3 is
   4 is
   5 finishes
   6 are you doing
   7 'll go
   8 'm meeting
   9 are you doing
  10 'm going
  11 are you leaving
  12 leaves
  13 Are you going
  14 'll take

3 1 how many nights it is
   2 if the trips are included in the price
   3 if all the rooms have showers
   4 how far it is from the station
   5 if we can visit Pompeii

4 1 her Italian was better now
   2 what Capri was
   3 if she had
   4 what she thought of
   5 wanted to visit Italy

5 1 *correct*
   2 where the exhibition is
   3 *correct*
   4 as soon as I get
   5 what I did
   6 where the town hall is
   7 *correct*
   8 as you come

Unit 4

1 1 b
   2 a

2 I often have difficulty with phrasal verbs.

3 2 does she usually have
   3 has / has got
   4 haven't got / don't have
   5 had
   6 had

7 doesn't have / hasn't got

8 'm having

Unit 5

1 1 a

2 a

2 Yes I went there when I was a student.

3 2 *correct*

3 *correct*

4 I worked

5 for ages

6 I've never eaten

7 *correct*

8 did Shakespeare write

Unit 6

1 1 a

2 a

2 Two years ago I went to Greece. I sailed around the islands.

3 2 had never lived

3 've missed

4 had left

5 arrived; had stopped

6 rang

7 realised; had forgotten

8 had changed

Test 2

1 1 this month

2 last week

3 last month

4 three years ago

5 so far today

2 1 Which school did you go to?

2 Have you got a driving licence?

3 How long have you been a qualified solicitor?

4 Have you ever worked in media law before?

5 How long did you work at City & Co.?

6 Had you ever been to China before 1994?

7 What did you study at university?

8 How long was your degree course?

3 1 left

2 went

3 had never worked

4 didn't know

5 found

6 decided

7 arrived

8 phoned

9 wasn't

10 told

11 had gone

12 felt

13 hadn't told

14 stayed

15 went

16 found

17 had come

18 got

19 had flown

4 1 've broken

2 've

3 waited

4 stated

5 went

6 started

7 've known

8 went

Unit 7

1 1 b

2 a

2 I must do more exercise.

3 2 had

3 must

4 having

5 must

6 have

7 had

8 have

Unit 8

1 1 b

2 a

2 It's Sunday. I don't have to get up.

3 2 mustn't
    3 mustn't
    4 don't have to
    5 mustn't
    6 don't have to
    7 don't have to
    8 mustn't

Unit 9

1 1 b
    2 b
2 Could I borrow your suntan oil, please?
3 2 *correct*
    3 were able to
    4 hasn't been able to
    5 Can / Could
    6 will probably be able to
    7 *correct*
    8 won't be able to

Test 3

1 1 c
    2 d
    3 f
    4 e
    5 a
    6 b
2 1 could
    2 wasn't able
    3 mustn't
    4 doesn't have to
    5 don't have to
    6 Can; have to
    7 couldn't / wasn't able to
3 1 mustn't
    2 don't have to
    3 have to
    4 mustn't
    5 have to
    6 can / am able to
    7 will be able to / can
    8 will be able
    9 can
    10 having to

4 1 mustn't take
    2 have to take a
    3 couldn't get / buy
    4 don't have to complete
    5 be able to leave
    6 must ask me
    7 wasn't able to
    8 mustn't / can't wear jeans
5 1 We couldn't see the Roman Baths.
    2 We had to pay to get in.
    3 We didn't have to buy tickets.
    4 They had to cancel the concert.
    5 We couldn't get tickets for the pottery exhibition.
    6 We didn't have to ask for permission.
    7 We couldn't understand the tour.
    8 We had to catch the train home.

Unit 10

1 1 a
    2 b
2 She said she would be slightly late. / She told me she would be slightly late.
3 2 say
    3 telling
    4 tells
    5 saying
    6 told
    7 says; tells
    8 tell

Unit 11

1 1 a
    2 a
2 I do a lot of exercise.
3 2 making
    3 do
    4 made
    5 make
    6 do
    7 made
    8 doing

Unit 12

1 1 a
    2 a

2 After driving for several hours we found a beautiful beach.

3 2 brought up
   3 *correct*
   4 take off
   5 *correct*
   6 grown
   7 find
   8 *correct*

Test 4

1 1 told Kerry to telephone him
   2 said she didn't want to
   3 told Nick she didn't like
   4 make another photocopy of
   5 make any noise
   6 you find out his
   7 make an effort
   8 do my best to

2 1 tell her
   2 They made
   3 *correct*
   4 took off
   5 *correct*
   6 found out
   7 making mistakes
   8 take off

3 1 did
   2 do
   3 tell
   4 says
   5 made
   6 make
   7 find out
   8 made

4 1 took off
   2 brought up
   3 grown up
   4 find out
   5 made up
   6 take off
   7 find out
   8 making up

5 1 telling
   2 told

3 do
4 said
5 found out
6 did
7 made up
8 making

Unit 13

1 1 a
   2 b

2 Her hair is not as long as mine.

3 2 like
   3 as
   4 like
   5 as
   6 like
   7 like
   8 like

Unit 14

1 1 b
   2 b

2 I have a lot of luggage.

3 2 doing research
   3 *correct*
   4 two jobs
   5 student accommodation is
   6 all this equipment
   7 some new software
   8 *correct*

Unit 15

1 1 b
   2 a

2 She plays football well.

3 2 well
   3 well
   4 well
   5 good; well
   6 well
   7 good
   8 well

Test 5

1 1 well
2 good
3 good
4 good
5 well
6 good
7 good
8 well
2 1 an
2 luggage
3 information
4 job
5 is
6 –
7 –
8 some
3 1 as
2 like
3 like
4 as
5 information
6 like
7 scenery
8 some
4 1 me some advice
2 he played tennis
3 your mother look like
4 looks like
5 with experience
6 well-known
7 as a waitress
8 some information

5 1 provide accommodation
2 give me some advice on
3 are the facilities like
4 do research in a specialist field
5 give me some information on postgraduate courses
6 What's their website like?
7 Is (Manchester) as big as
8 he look like now

Unit 16

1 1 a
2 a
2 The dog's chasing its tail.
3 2 It's very vicious
3 Who's; children's
4 women's; children's
5 They've; name's
6 don't; it's too small; doesn't
7 There's
8 friend's

Unit 17

1 1 a
2 b
2 It gets very cold here in winter.
3 2 letting agencies, or you …
3 December; Christmas; New Year
4 Jack's; Range Rover
5 Chief Executive
6 Emma Roberts; Thames
7 so far, but …
8 University, but …

Unit 18

1 1 a
2 b
2 Emma's pay increase was very disappointing.
3 2 accommodation
3 definitely
4 environment
5 government
6 really
7 wonderful
8 comfortable

Test 6

1 writing; accommodation; centre; which; really; beautiful; grateful; advertisement; comfortable; definitely
2 1 people's
2 really disappointed

3 students'
4 it's
5 years
6 courgettes, aubergines, peppers(,) and tomatoes (final comma is optional)
7 summer; August
8 cancelled

3 1 sister's
  2 sisters'
  3 *correct*
  4 Luke's; children's
  5 I'm; it's
  6 *correct*
  7 I'm; children's
  8 It's a good film; can't

4 1 advertisement
  2 accommodation
  3 bicycle
  4 comfortably
  5 definitely
  6 preferred
  7 beginning
  8 disappointing

5 Pyramids; Pharaohs, but; future, and; that it's; World; years (no apostrophe); Egypt; it's unlikely

Unit 19
1 1 b
  2 a
2 I love walking in the countryside.
3 2 countryside
  3 environment
  4 journey
  5 trip
  6 way
  7 nature
  8 environment

Unit 20
1 1 b
  2 b
2 Sam is very irritable when he's just woken up.
3 2 irritable

3 boring
4 funny
5 surprised
6 nervous
7 fun
8 interested

Unit 21
1 1 b
  2 b
2 I need to get to the station in ten minutes! My train leaves at 1.30!
3 2 go
  3 go
  4 get
  5 get
  6 get to know
  7 get
  8 take

Test 7
1 1 bored
  2 angry
  3 fun
  4 countryside
  5 embarrassed
  6 environment
  7 interesting
  8 fun
2 1 go
  2 get
  3 journey
  4 way
  5 go
  6 irritable
  7 countryside
  8 fun
3 1 always have fun
  2 takes four hours to get
  3 the film (very) funny
  4 got to know a few
  5 journey to Delhi is
  6 (very) surprised to hear
  7 always have fun in his
  8 was disappointed with
4 1 bored

2 interested
3 fun
4 surprised
5 embarrassing
6 disappointed
7 irritable
8 boring

5 1 to get
2 the journey
3 bored
4 *correct*
5 She gets nervous
6 can I get
7 *correct*
8 can be fun

Unit 22

1 1 b
2 a

2 I hope you have a wonderful time here!

3 2 wish I had worked harder
3 wish I could come
4 wish I didn't have to
5 hope you win
6 hope she enjoyed / hope she's enjoyed
7 wish you would stop
8 hope she arrives

Unit 23

1 1 b
2 a

2 At first, I didn't like eating snails but now I enjoy them.

3 2 *correct*
3 firstly
4 In my opinion,
5 On the other hand,
6 *correct*
7 *correct*
8 At first

Unit 24

1 1 b
2 a

2 I saw the car in your advertisement.

3 2 in
3 to
4 in; in
5 to
6 in
7 to
8 to

Test 8

1 1 first I didn't like
2 my opinion, it's not / it isn't
3 wish you wouldn't ask
4 looking forward to seeing
5 hope you had
6 of all, preheat the oven
7 the other hand,
8 wish I had worked harder

2 1 *correct*
2 in Spanish
3 in all the newspapers
4 *correct*
5 explained to
6 listen to
7 in that advertisement
8 forward to

3 1 of
2 According
3 hope
4 to
5 wish
6 hope
7 in
8 hope

4 1 hope
2 in
3 wish
4 in
5 to
6 according
7 to
8 hope

5 1 in English
2 in all the newspapers
3 According to

4 write to us
5 on the contrary
6 *correct*
7 in July
8 forward to

Unit 25
1 1 b
   2 a
2 I can still remember when you were this high!
3 2 He's still looking
   3 She's already seen
   4 she can already read
   5 paid him for it yet
   6 They're still looking
   7 He's already spent
   8 fixed it yet

Unit 26
1 1 b
   2 a
2 Don't worry! The exam will be very easy!
3 2 too late
   3 –
   4 very strong
   5 busy enough
   6 too embarrassed
   7 fantastic
   8 too much; enough food

Unit 27
1 1 b
   2 b
2 Despite their bad behaviour Amy adores her nephews.
3 2 keen on
   3 depends on
   4 experience of
   5 *correct*
   6 *correct*
   7 *correct*
   8 Most of

Test 9
1 1 was astonished

2 depends on
3 *correct*
4 enough money
5 very tired
6 Most of the staff
7 *correct*
8 *correct*
2 1 already spoken to you
   2 your room still
   3 got there they had already
   4 haven't had breakfast yet
   5 depends on my boss whether
   6 wore his jacket despite
   7 most people put
   8 have enough time to
3 1 still
   2 yet
   3 still
   4 already
   5 on
   6 –
   7 very
   8 –
4 1 already
   2 yet
   3 –
   4 on
   5 very
   6 still
   7 –
   8 –
5 1 I like cricket but I'm not fond of football.
   2 No, I think most people will like it.
   3 I've never had previous experience of acting.
   4 Despite the long hours I enjoy it.
   5 No, I don't have enough time for a girlfriend!
   6 We've already started a sequel.
   7 Most of my friends are very happy for me.
   8 It depends on the success of this film.

Unit 28

1   1   a
    2   b
2   Can you take a photo of us?
3   2   take
    3   bring
    4   take care of
    5   take advantage of
    6   take
    7   pays attention
    8   profit from

Unit 29

1   1   b
    2   a
2   I'm often too busy to have lunch.
3   2   *correct*
    3   *correct*
    4   *correct*
    5   of the pollution
    6   and the music
    7   *correct*
    8   The work

Unit 30

1   1   a
    2   b
2   As soon as Ryan sent the joke email to his boss he regretted it.
3   2   *correct*
    3   stand it
    4   *correct*
    5   regret it
    6   believe it
    7   prefer it
    8   *correct*

Test 10

1   1   Kindness
    2   lunch
    3   work
    4   the pollution
    5   money
    6   the money
    7   Unemployment
    8   the Internet
2   1   take a break
    2   take advantage of
    3   on the Internet
    4   I love history
    5   *correct*
    6   can't bear it
    7   enjoy it
    8   get the visa
3   1   to take advantage of
    2   take some
    3   to pay attention to
    4   to take me
    5   attention to him
    6   *correct*
    7   take advantage of
    8   take care of
4   1   –
    2   advantage
    3   profit
    4   of
    5   it
    6   it
    7   bring
    8   –
5   1   takes care of
    2   pay attention to
    3   can't stand it when
    4   'd appreciate it if
    5   I still find it
    6   enjoyed it
    7   finds archaeology fascinating
    8   regret it

Acknowledgements

I would like to thank my editors, Anna Teevan and Helen Forrest, for all their comments and advice.

The author and publishers would also like to thank Clare West and Gregory Manin, who commented on the material in its draft form.

The Cambridge Learner Corpus
This book is based on information from the Cambridge Learner Corpus, a collection of over 45,000 exam papers from Cambridge ESOL. It shows real mistakes students make, and highlights which parts of English cause particular problems for learners.

The Cambridge Learner Corpus has been developed jointly with the University of Cambridge ESOL Examinations and forms part of the Cambridge International Corpus.

To find out more, visit
www.cambridge.org/elt/corpus